JAN -- 1993   L I

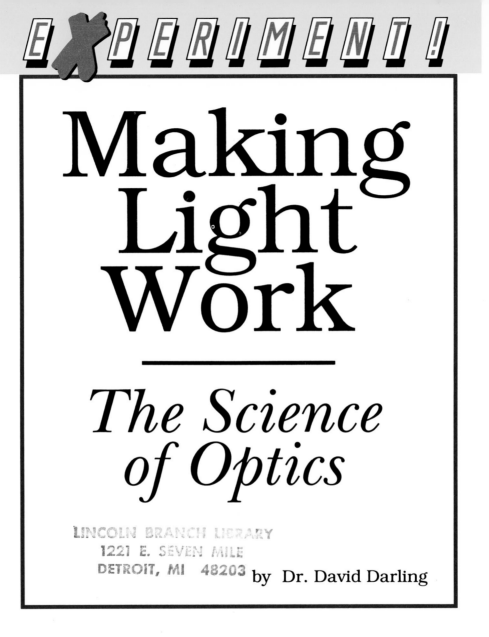

EXPERIMENT!

Making Light Work

The Science of Optics

by Dr. David Darling

 DILLON PRESS
New York

Maxwell Macmillan Canada
Toronto

Maxwell Macmillan International
New York Oxford Singapore Sydney

Photographic Acknowledgments

The photographs are reproduced through the courtesy of the National Astronomy and Ionosphere Center, NASA, and Unicorn Stock Photos/ Robert W. Ginn, J. Risley.

Library of Congress Cataloging-in-Publication Data
Darling, David J.
    Making light work : the science of optics / by David Darling.
        p. cm. — (Experiment!)
    Includes index.
    Summary: Demonstrates the principles of optics and light through a variety of experiments.
    ISBN 0-87518-476-6
    1. Optics—Juvenile literature. 2. Optics—Experiments—Juvenile literature. [1. Optics—Experiments. 2. Light—Experiments. 3. Experiments.] I. Title. II. Series: Darling, David J. Experiment!
QC360.D37 1991
535—dc20
                                        91-3999

Dillon Press
Macmillan Publishing Company
866 Third Avenue
New York, NY 10022

Maxwell Macmillan Canada, Inc.
1200 Eglinton Avenue East
Suite 200
Don Mills, Ontario M3C 3N1

Macmillan Publishing Company is part of the Maxwell Communication Group of Companies.

First edition
Printed in the United States of America
10 9 8 7 6 5 4 3 2 1

Contents

What Is Science?

Imagine gazing to the edge of the universe with the help of a giant telescope, or designing a future car using a computer that can do over a billion calculations a second. Think what it would be like to investigate the strange calls of the humpback whale, dig up the bones of a new type of dinosaur, or drill a hole ten miles into the earth.

As you read this, men and women around the world are doing exactly these things. Others are trying to find out how the human brain works, how to build better rocket engines, and how to develop new energy sources for the twenty-first century. There are researchers working at the South Pole, in the Amazon jungle, under the sea, in space, and in laboratories on every continent. All these people are scientists. But what does that mean? Just what is science?

Observation

Science is simply a way of looking at the world with an open, inquiring mind. It usually starts with an observation. For example, you might observe that the leaves of some trees turn brown, yellow, or red in fall. That may seem obvious. But

to a scientist, it raises all sorts of interesting questions. What substances in a leaf cause the various colors? What happens when the color changes? Does the leaf swap its green-colored chemical for a brown one? Or are the chemicals that cause the fall colors there all the time but remain hidden from view when the green substance is present?

Hypothesis

At this stage, you might come up with your own explanation for what is going on inside the leaf. This early explanation–a sort of intelligent guess–is called a working hypothesis. To be useful, a hypothesis should lead to predictions that can be tested. For instance, your hypothesis might be that leaves always contain brown, yellow, or red chemicals. It is just that when the green substance is there it masks or covers over the other colors. This is a good scientific hypothesis because a test can be done that could prove it wrong.

Experiment

As a next step, you might devise an experiment to look more deeply into the problem. A well-designed experiment allows you to isolate the factors you think are important, while controlling or leaving out the rest.

Somehow you have to extract the colored chemicals from a batch of green

leaves and those from a batch of brown leaves. You might do this, for example, by crushing the leaves and putting a drop of "leaf juice" partway up a narrow strip of blotting paper. Hanging the blotting paper so that it dips in a bowl of water would then cause different colored chemicals from the leaf to be carried to different heights up the paper. By comparing the blotting paper records from the green leaves and the brown leaves, you would be able to tell which chemicals were the same and which were different. Then, depending on the results, you could conclude either that your first hypothesis seemed right or that it needed to be replaced.

Real Science

What we have just described is perhaps the "standard" or "ideal" way to do science. But just as real houses are never spotlessly clean, real science is never quite as neat and tidy as we might wish. Experiments and investigations do not always go the

way scientists expect. Being human, scientists cannot control all the parts of an experiment. Sometimes they are surprised by the results, and often important discoveries are made completely by chance.

Breakthroughs in science do not even have to begin with an observation of the outside world. Albert Einstein, for instance, used "thought experiments" as the starting point for his greatest pieces of work—the special and general theories of relativity. One of his earliest thought experiments was to imagine what it would be like to ride on a light beam. The fact is, scientists use all sorts of different approaches, depending on the problem and the circumstances.

Some important things, however, are common to all science. First, scientists must always be ready to admit mistakes or that their knowledge is incomplete. Scientific ideas are thrown out and replaced if they no longer agree with what is observed. There is no final "truth" in science–only an ongoing quest for better and better explanations of the real world.

Second, all good experiments must be able to be repeated so that other scientists can check the results. It is always possible to make an error, especially in a complicated experiment. So, it is essential that other people, in other places, can perform the same experiment to see if they agree with the findings.

Third, to be effective, science must be shared. In other words, scientists from all over the world must exchange their ideas and results freely through journals and meetings. Not only that, but the general public must be kept informed of what scientists are doing so that they, too, can help to shape the future of scientific research.

To become a better scientist yourself is quite simple. Keep an open mind, ask lots of questions, and most important of all—experiment!

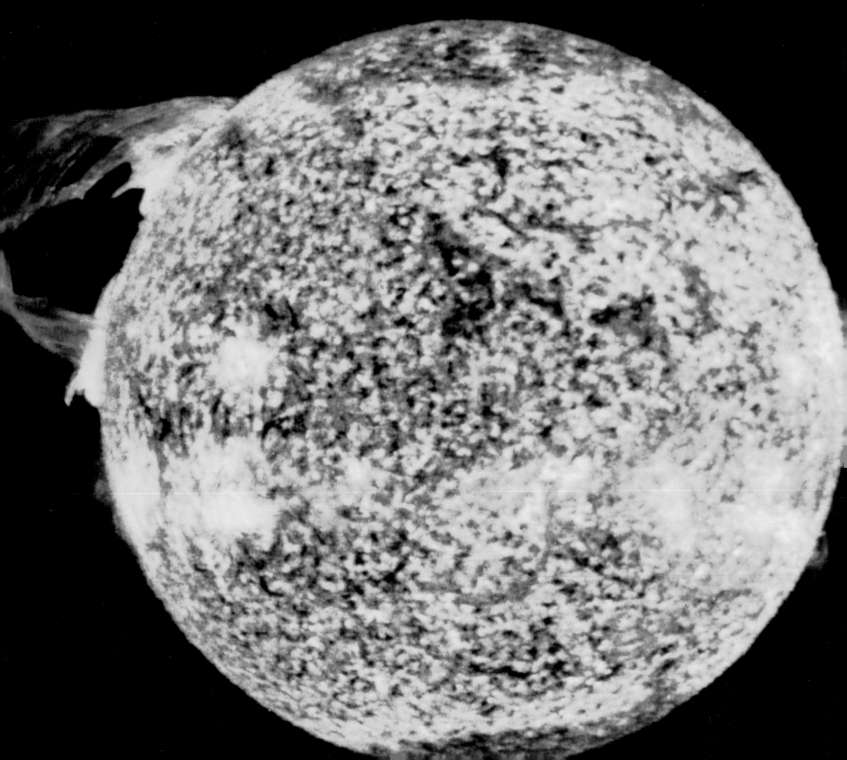

CHAPTER 1

Light Rays and Shadow Plays

What do rainbows, glowworms, candles, telescopes, and compact disk players have in common? The answer is that they all depend in some way upon light.

Light is not a form of matter–a solid, liquid, or gas. It cannot be held or stored. Yet it *can* cause change. It can affect the chemicals in a photographic film so that a picture appears on the film. It can also cause changes in the sensitive layer at the back of our eyes, enabling us to see. When any change takes place, energy is involved. So, light is a form of energy.

The biggest, brightest source of every-day light is the sun. Traveling at 186,282 miles per second–the highest speed in the universe–light takes 8 1/3 minutes to cross the 93-million-mile gap between the sun and earth.

Light from more distant objects takes longer to reach us. For example, if you look at the brightest star in the night sky, Sirius, you see it as it was 8 years ago. Because it takes light time to reach us, the farther we look into space, the farther we look back in time.

Light and Matter

Light can travel through empty space, and it can also travel through certain kinds of matter. Substances such as glass, water, and air, which let light pass right through them, are called transparent.

Other materials, including frosted glass, tracing paper, and uncut diamonds, allow only some light to pass through. They are said to be translucent. Still other substances block out all the light that falls on them and are called opaque.

Most objects do not give off any light

◀ *The sun is the biggest and brightest source of light on earth.*

Making Shadows

You Will Need:

- **A bright light (The beam of a slide projector works especially well.)**
- **A large piece of white cardboard**
- **A 12" ruler**
- **Several regular-shaped solids—for example, a cube, oblong box, sphere, pyramid, cylinder, and cone**

What to Do:

Fix the cardboard upright against a wall. With the room darkened, shine the light at the cardboard. Hold a solid object, such as your hand or a book, in front of the cardboard. Look at the shadow that is cast. What happens to the size of the shadow as you move the object, first nearer and then farther away from the light?

Make two marks on the cardboard two feet apart. Start with the 12" ruler against the cardboard and move it toward the source of light until the shadow of the ruler just stretches between the two marks. Measure the distance from the ruler to the light and the distance from the cardboard to the light. Divide the first measurement by the second. To double the size of the shadow, what do you have to do to the ruler's distance from the light source? What would you have to do to make the shadow four times bigger?

Take one of the regular-shaped solids and cast its shadow. Turn the object slowly around. What happens to the shadow? Remember, the shape of the shadow is the same as the outline of the object as seen from the direction of the light. Try the other regular-shaped solids and see how many different regular-shaped shadows you can create from them. For example, from a cone you should be able to make a circle and a triangle. Record your findings in a table.

Taking It Further:

Start with an object almost touching the screen. Look closely at the edge of the shadow. Now gradually move the object toward the light. What happens to the edge of the shadow? Invent a hypothesis to explain your observation.

For more about this experiment, see "Experiment in Depth," pages 52-53, section 1.

of their own. We can see them only by the light they reflect from the sun or from artificial sources such as electric lights and candle flames.

Light and Shadows

The next time you go to the movies and the action begins on the screen, turn your back on it for a moment. Look in the direction of the projector. Particles of dust in the air scatter some of the light from the projector so that you can see the beam. Notice that the beam is straight. Light always travels along the most direct path that it can.

An opaque object blocks the light that falls on it. Everywhere else, the light continues in a straight path until it bounces off the ground or wall behind. The result is a dark patch, or shadow, with the same outline as the object, surrounded by light.

▲ *Photographers use different types of lights in a studio.*

A Photographer's Studio

If you have your picture taken in a studio, you will notice that the photographer uses a variety of different lights. Two or more floodlights are set up to light you equally from both sides, so that no shadows fall on your face. These floodlights shine backward into an umbrellalike reflector that produces a broad, even beam.

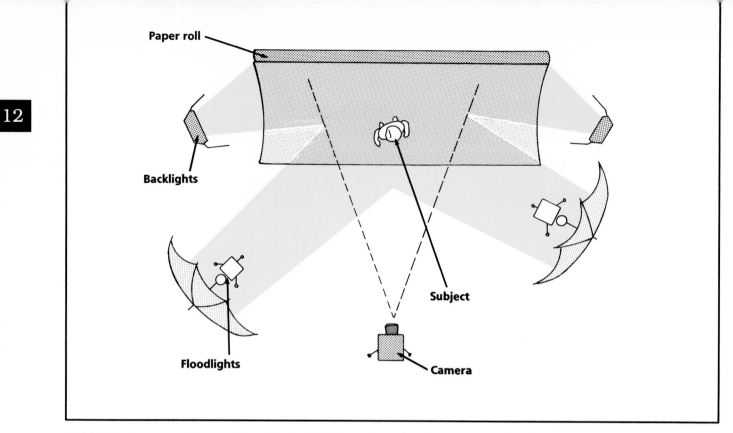

Paper roll

Backlights

Floodlights

Subject

Camera

▲ *Lights in a studio are directed at different angles to remove shadows.*

In addition, two or more "backlights" are placed on each side of you. These shine directly onto the screen behind you to remove shadows the floodlights cast. A similar though more complicated arrangement of lights is used when photographing fashion models indoors or shooting movies on a studio set.

Eclipses

The moon and the sun seem to be almost exactly the same size as seen from earth. This is because although the sun is about 400 times bigger than the moon, it is also about 400 times farther away.

As a result, when the moon passes directly between the sun and earth, it just

Viewed from Plymouth, Massachusetts, in ▶ June 1984, this solar eclipse blocked out 92 percent of the sun's light.

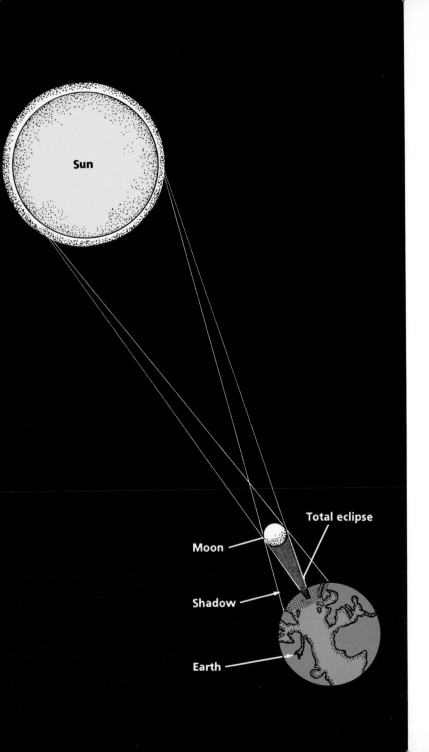

Sun

Total eclipse

Moon

Shadow

Earth

covers the sun's bright face. From certain places on earth, the sun is blocked out and the sky grows dark. This is called a total solar eclipse. For a few minutes, someone standing in the shadow cast by the moon can glimpse the faint outer atmosphere of the sun. Then the moon's shadow races on, making a track across the earth only a few hundred miles wide.

Believe It or Not!

TO EARTH (STILL UNDER CONSTRUCTION)

LIGHT FROM THE MOST DISTANT OBJECT EVER SEEN BEGAN ITS JOURNEY TO EARTH OVER 15 BILLION YEARS AGO—LONG BEFORE THE EARTH EXISTED.

◄ *This diagram shows how the moon blocks out the light from the sun during a solar eclipse.*

CHAPTER 2

Through the Looking Glass

As Alice found in Lewis Carrolls' famous story, there are many surprises waiting through the looking glass. Mirrors are not only useful, they are fun to experiment with as well.

All substances reflect, or bounce back, some of the light that falls on them. But usually the light is scattered in all directions so that the surface appears dull. If the reflecting surface is very smooth and polished, however, it bounces the light back in a regular way. It acts as a mirror.

Mirror, Mirror, on the Wall

Glass can be made very flat and smooth. But it does not reflect well. It bounces back only about one-twentieth of the light that falls on it. However, you can turn a window pane into a mirror simply by taping a piece of aluminum foil to one side of the glass. Looking from the other side of the window you will now see a reflection of yourself. It is a fairly poor reflection because the foil does not fit closely enough to the flat surface of the glass.

Proper mirrors are not made by using foil but by coating the back of a piece of glass directly with metal. Silver is normally used because it reflects well and there is a process by which it can be applied easily to glass as a thin, even layer. The glass gives a smooth surface for the silver to cling to and also protects the silver from tarnishing.

Reflections and Images

The reflection of an object in a mirror is called an image. An image always appears to be the same distance behind a flat mirror as the object is in front.

▲ The smooth, polished windows of a skyscraper reflect the image of nearby buildings.

The Topsy-Turvy World of Mirrors

You Will Need:

- **A mirror**
- **A ruler**
- **A second mirror***
- **A protractor***
  Note: items marked "*" are used only in the "Taking It Further" part of an experiment.

What to Do:

Look at yourself in the mirror. Raise your right hand. Which hand does the person in the mirror lift? The mirror seems to swap right for left. But why does it not also swap top for bottom? Look more closely. Your right hand is still the same hand in the mirror. What the mirror has really done is turn your hand around front to back.

Place a ruler so that one end is touching the mirror as shown in the diagram. Notice that the reflection of the ruler in the mirror is pointing in the opposite direction. Now, place your finger next to the line showing 6". What is the finger in the mirror pointing at? Point at the line showing 9" and check what the mirror finger is doing. What can you deduce about the distances of objects and their reflections on either side of the mirror?

Taking It Further:

To see yourself as other people see you requires two mirrors. Set up the mirrors at right angles. Now your reflection in the first mirror is reflected again in the second mirror. This turns all your features, your hair part, and so on, the right way round so that they appear as in real life.

Look at your "real life" reflection and try to touch your left eye with your right hand. If you have difficulty, why do you think this should be?

Arrange the two mirrors so that they are facing one another with your head in between. Try to explain what you see.

Using the protractor, set up the mirrors so they make angles of 60 degrees, 45 degrees, and 30 degrees. Describe the number and type of reflections you see.

A Beam Tank

You Will Need:

- **A slide projector or other very bright source of light**
- **A piece of cardboard that is opaque to your light source**
- **A large clear glass container with upright sides, such as a fish tank or laboratory water bath**
- **Two small mirrors (The type dentists use for examining teeth works well.)**

What to Do:

Partly fill the container with water and add a few drops of milk to produce a slightly cloudy mixture. Place the container on a dark surface. Position the light source about a foot away from the container so that the beam shines level through the water.

Poke a number of small holes in the cardboard so that when the cardboard is placed in front of the beam the light shines through. Set up the cardboard at the side of the tank facing the beam. Darken the room as much as possible. Look down from directly above the tank and you should see several narrow beams of light.

Hold a mirror upright in the path of the narrow beams. What happens as you alter the angle the mirror makes to the incoming light?

Introduce the second mirror so that it stands upright in the path of the reflected beam from the first. Observe what happens as you turn this second mirror. Turn both mirrors at once to control the direction of the final beam.

Taking It Further:

Suggest and investigate ways in which your beam tank could be improved.

For more about this, see "Experiment in Depth," page 53, section 2.

▼ *What happens to light as it shines through the beam tank into two small mirrors?*

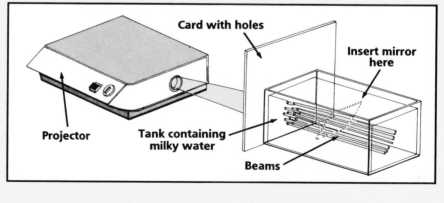

Card with holes

Insert mirror here

Projector

Tank containing milky water

Beams

Ray Tracing

You Will Need:

- **A large flat wooden or cork board covered with a sheet of white paper**
- **A large flat mirror**
- **Pins**
- **A ruler**
- **A pencil**
- **A protractor**

What to Do:

Support the mirror securely so that it stands upright at the back of the board. Stick two pins upright in the board so that you can see their reflections in the mirror. Line up the images of the two pins and stick two more pins in the board exactly along this line.

Remove all the pins. Draw a line to the mirror that passes through the holes made by the first two pins. This represents an incoming ray of light. Draw another line from the mirror that passes through the holes made by the second two pins. This follows the track of the reflected or outgoing ray. Use the protractor to measure the angle between the incoming ray and the mirror and the angle between the outgoing ray and the mirror.

Repeat the experiment with pins in different positions. Record your results on a chart. What do you conclude?

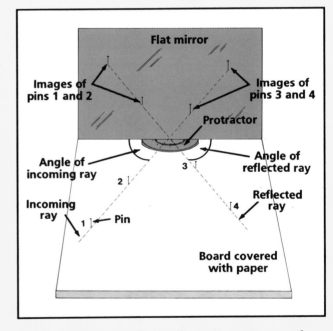

▲ *This diagram shows how to measure the angle of an incoming and outgoing ray of light.*

Glancing Rays

You Will Need:

- **The beam tank**
- **A microscope slide, or other small piece of flat clear glass**

What to Do:
Place the slide so that it is at right angles to the light rays in the tank. What happens to the rays?

Slowly rotate the slide. Notice what happens when the incoming rays meet the slide at a small glancing angle. Observe closely and describe what you see. How do your findings relate to the subject of optical fibers described below?

Equal Angles
When you throw a ball at a smooth wall, it bounces off at the same angle as it hits. The same is true of light striking a flat mirror. Light rays are reflected from a mirror at the same angle as they arrive.

Optical Fibers

A transparent or translucent material will reflect most of the light falling on it if the light approaches the surface of the material at a small enough angle. This fact makes it possible to send light for very long distances through narrow, flexible strands of glass called optical fibers. Light from a bright source travels along an optical fiber in a zigzag path. Instead of escaping, it hits the sides of the fiber at a small angle and is reflected back inside.

In parts of the United States and other countries, optical fibers are already being used to carry phone conversations in the

A close-up view of light ▶ passing through an optical fiber.

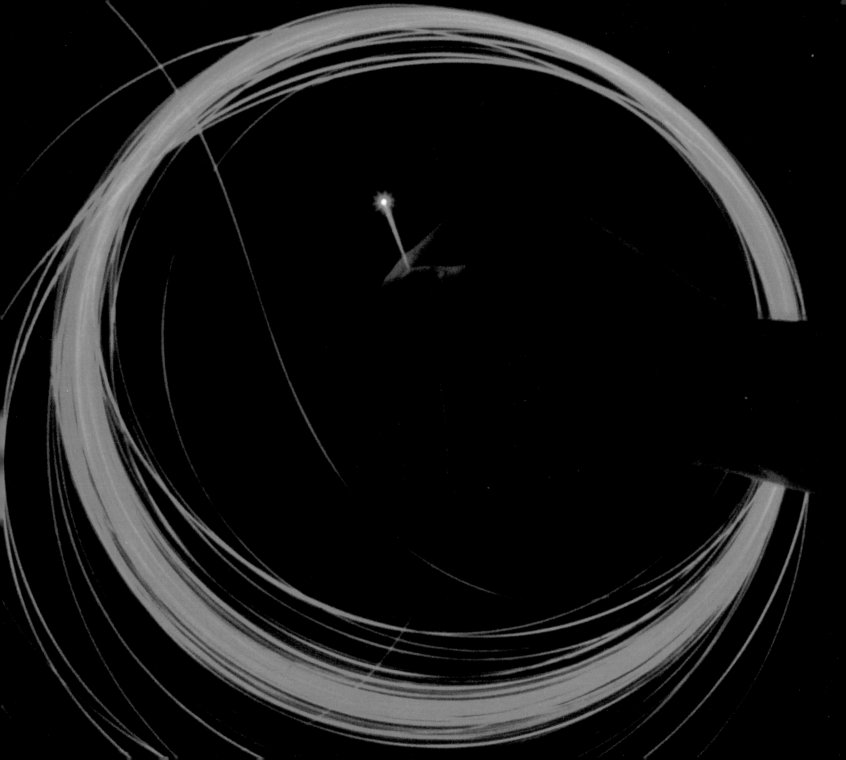

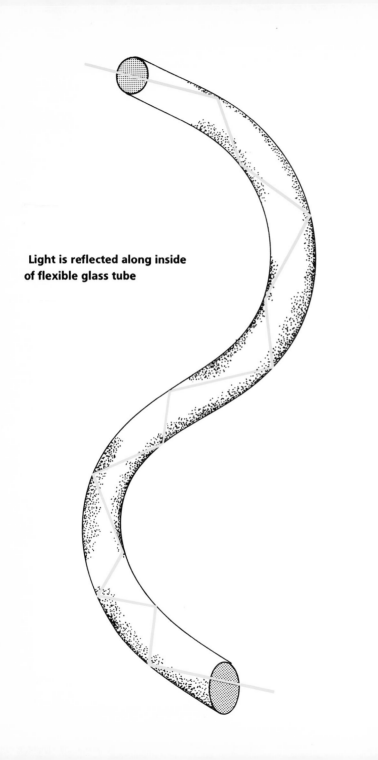

Light is reflected along inside of flexible glass tube

form of tiny flashes of light. A bundle of optical fibers, no thicker than your little finger, can carry 10,000 phone calls at once—more than a copper cable the thickness of your arm is capable of carrying.

◀ *Light travels along an optical fiber by bouncing from side to side along the fiber.*

Liquid Light

You Will Need:

- A bright flashlight
- A plastic soft drink bottle
- A plastic bowl
- A sheet of black cardboard
- Sticky tape
- Scissors

What to Do:

Cut the bottle in half and wrap the black cardboard around the lower half, securing it with sticky tape. Make a hole with the end of the scissors about 3" from the bottom of the bottle. Place the bottle in the bowl. Darken the room. Fill the bottle with water and shine the flashlight into the bottle.

Observe what happens. Try to explain what you see in terms of the way optical fibers work. How can you tell that the escaping water is not a very good optical fiber?

For more about this experiment, see "Experiment in Depth," page 54, section 3.

Caution: Take care when using scissors. Never point them toward you.

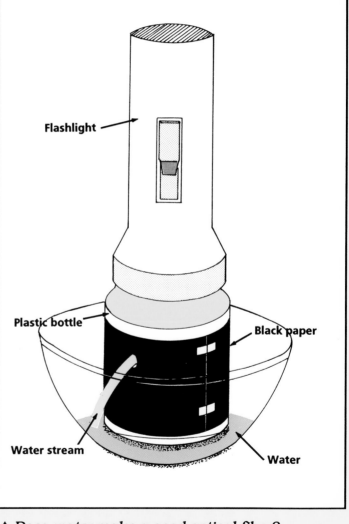

Flashlight

Plastic bottle

Black paper

Water stream

Water

▲ *Does water make a good optical fiber?*

CHAPTER 3

In the Hall of Mirrors

A visit to the hall of mirrors at a fair will reveal two facts. First, not all mirrors are flat. And second, curved mirrors can do very strange things to your appearance!

A mirror that curves in from the edge to the middle is said to be concave. One that bulges out from the edge to the middle is called convex.

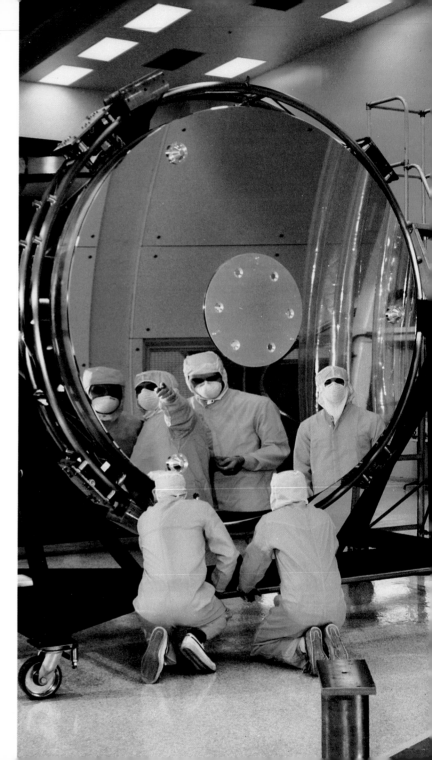

The image of NASA technicians ▶
is reflected in the main mirror
of the Hubble Space Telescope.

Reflections in a Spoon

You Will Need:

- A large, clean, unscratched spoon
- An ordinary flat mirror
- A 12" ruler
- The beam tank*
- Several different concave and convex mirrors*

What to Do:

The inside surface of the spoon acts as a concave mirror. Hold the spoon 12 inches in front of your face. Which way up is your reflection? Measure the height of the image of your head. Now replace the spoon with a flat mirror held in the same position. Measure the height of your head as seen in the flat mirror. Which image is larger? Divide the height of the image in the spoon by that in the flat mirror to find by how much your reflection has been shrunk or enlarged in the spoon. Finally, hold the spoon so that the concave side is almost touching your eye. What do you see? Which way up is the image? Is it smaller, larger, or the same as it would be in a flat mirror?

The outside surface of a spoon works as a convex mirror. Repeat all the steps just described with this side of the spoon.

Taking It Further:

Hold the spoon upright in the beam tank with the concave side facing the light. Observe what happened to the beams, both from above and from the side of the tank. Tilt the spoon in different directions. How does this affect the reflected beams? Repeat these steps using the convex side of the spoon.

If you can obtain proper concave and convex mirrors, experiment with these in the beam tank. How do the results differ from those using the spoon?

For more about this experiment, see "Experiment in Depth," page 54, section 4.

Uses of Curved Mirrors

A concave mirror can produce two types of images. When an object is placed quite far from the mirror, an image is formed that is upside down and reduced in size. When the object is brought close up, however, the concave mirror gives an image that is upright and magnified. In the case of a spoon, which is highly curved, objects almost have to touch the spoon for this magnified image to appear. But a mirror that curves more gently gives an upright, magnified image at a greater distance–say, a foot or two away. This makes it useful, for example, as a shaving mirror or a makeup mirror.

Concave mirrors are also used in large telescopes (see "The Hubble Space Telescope" on page 27). They allow a lot of light to be collected from the direction in which they are pointing, so that even very faint objects can be seen.

Convex mirrors, on the other hand, give

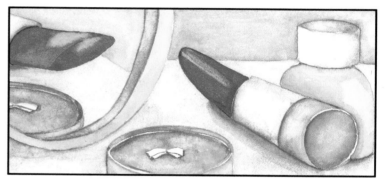

▲ *The side-view mirror of a car is a convex mirror, while a cosmetic mirror is concave.*

only one type of image–upright and reduced in size. Their advantage is that they can show objects spread over a wide area. This makes them useful as side-view mirrors on cars and trucks. A flat mirror would give a restricted view, but a convex mirror provides a view of most of the road behind the driver.

◀ *The* Hubble Space Telescope *has a large concave mirror to view faraway objects in space.*

The Hubble Space Telescope

One of the problems scientists face in trying to study the universe is that the earth's atmosphere gets in the way. Moving currents of air and dust blur the appearance of stars and other distant objects. As a result, telescopes on the earth's surface are limited in the amount of detail they can show.

It was a great step forward, therefore, when the *Hubble Space Telescope* was launched on April 24, 1990. This instrument now circles around the earth in an orbit 373 miles high, taking the clearest pictures of the universe ever seen. The most important part of the new telescope is a concave mirror measuring 98 inches across. This gathers the light from distant objects and concentrates it onto a smaller flat mirror, ready to be magnified.

Shortly after it was launched, scientists discovered a serious error in the spacing of two mirrors inside the *Hubble Space Telescope* that affects it ability to focus images. In 1993, this problem will be fixed during a planned maintenance visit by astronauts. Meanwhile, researchers are using computers to correct the images from the space telescope so that they appear sharper.

CHAPTER 4

When Light Bends

Spear fishermen use a strange trick to catch their prey. They aim at a point slightly *below* where the fish seems to be! The reason is that light changes direction when it moves from one transparent substance, such as water, to another of a different density, such as air. This change of direction is called refraction.

You can find many examples of refraction in everyday life. A bar of soap at the bottom of a bath appears to be higher than it really is. A pencil seen through the side of a water-filled jar seems to be broken. And a riverbed, seen from the bank, looks shallower than its true depth.

▲ *Light changes direction when it moves from air into water.*

Refraction in Action

You will need:

- **The beam tank**
- **A 12" ruler**

What to Do:

Lay down the ruler so that it extends from the light source to the base of the holed card. Line up the ruler with the center of the incoming light beam.

First, arrange for the light to come in at right angles to the card. Look down on the beam tank. Has anything happened to the direction of the light as the beam goes from air to water?

Now move the light source around to one side slightly so that the incoming beam is still pointing at the holes in the card but is no longer square on the card. Again, place the ruler so that it lies exactly along the center of the incoming beam. Look closely at the direction of the light after it has entered the water. What do you notice?

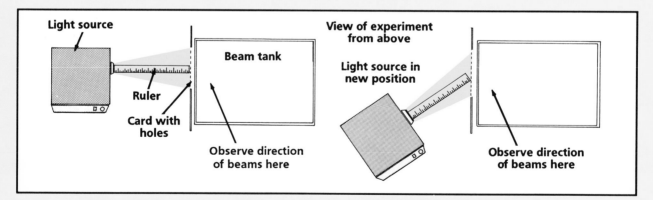

▲ *This diagram shows light entering the beam tank from two different angles.*

A Change of Course

Light travels faster through air than it does through a denser substance, such as water or glass. So, when light rays travel through air and meet the surface of the denser substance, they are suddenly slowed down. When this happens, the light rays bend. You can see a similar effect if you throw a stone at a slant into water. As it leaves the thinner air and enters the thicker water, it slows and is dragged on a more downward path. The only exception is when the incoming rays (or stone) meet the surface at right angles. In this case, there is no change of direction.

Mirages

On a hot day, you can sometimes see what looks like a pool of water on the ground—even though the ground is completely dry. In fact, the "pool" is caused by refracted light from the sky. The air close to the

▲ *Why does the straw appear to be bent as it enters a glass of water?*

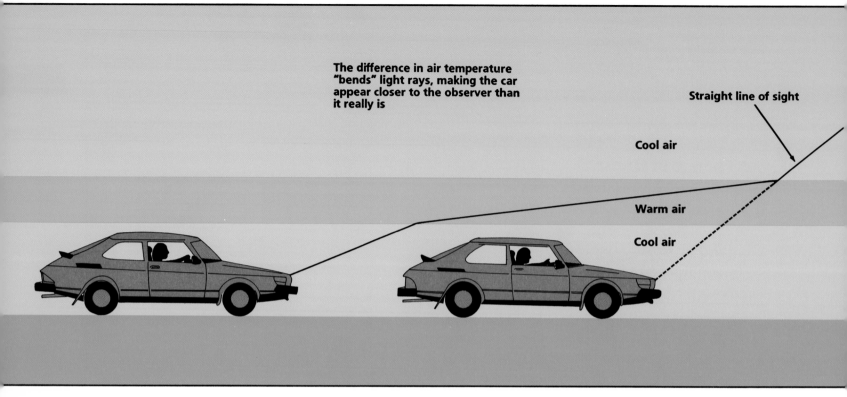

The difference in air temperature "bends" light rays, making the car appear closer to the observer than it really is

Straight line of sight

Cool air

Warm air

Cool air

▲ *As light passes through air of different temperatures, it is refracted and causes a mirage.*

ground becomes hotter and, therefore, less dense than the air higher up. This change in density causes light from the sky to be bent upward so that it reaches your eyes from the direction of the ground. The effect is called a mirage and is common on hot roads and in deserts. As well as the sky, mirages of distant objects on the horizon such as mountains may be seen.

Believe It or Not!

ON JULY 17, 1939, A MIRAGE OF THE 4,715-FOOT ICELANDIC MOUNTAIN SNAEFELLS JOKULL WAS SEEN AT SEA FROM A DISTANCE OF 335 MILES!

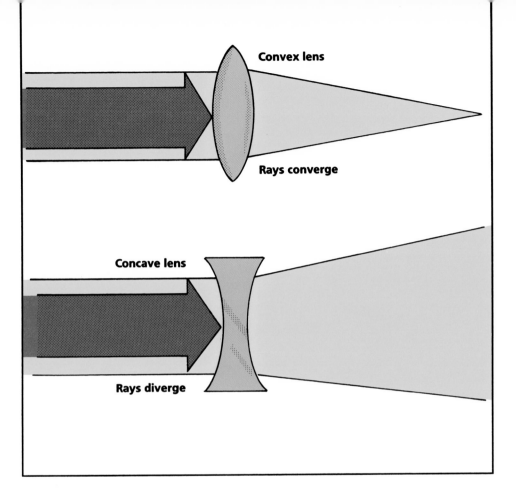

Convex lens

Rays converge

Concave lens

Rays diverge

◀ *This diagram shows how convex and concave lenses bend light as it passes through them.*

Lenses

Refraction can be put to good use by shaping pieces of glass so that one or both sides are smoothly curved. These curved pieces of glass are called lenses. As light passes through them it is bent in a special way, following a certain order.

Just as there are convex and concave mirrors, so there are convex and concave lenses. In a convex lens, the glass bulges out from the edge to the center, while in a concave lens it curves the other way.

Lens Power

You Will Need:

- **A convex lens, such as that in a magnifying glass**
- **A concave lens, such as those in spectacles of people who cannot see distant objects clearly**
- **A 12" ruler**
- **A piece of white cardboard**
- **The beam tank***

What to Do:

Hold the convex lens a few inches above the words on the page. Do the words look bigger, smaller, or the same size? Are they upright or not? Measure how far the lens can be placed from the page before the letters start to become blurred. Call this measurement A.

Now put the convex lens upright about six feet away from a source of light such as an electric light bulb. Let the light that passes through the lens fall onto the white cardboard. Move the cardboard (or the lens) until you obtain a small, sharp image of the light source on the cardboard. Measure the distance from the lens to the cardboard. This distance is known as the focal length of the lens. Call it measurement

B. Compare measurements A and B. Which is greater?

Hold the convex lens at arm's length and look at a distant object. What do you observe? Does the object look larger, smaller, or the same size? Which way up is it?

Now take the concave lens. Hold it a few inches from this page. What effect does it have on the words? What happens as you move it farther and farther from the page? Do the words eventually become blurred as they did with the convex lens? Hold the concave lens at arm's length and look at a distant object. What do you observe?

Taking It Further:

Hold the convex lens upright in the beam tank in the path of the light rays. Look down from above and from the side. What do you observe? Measure the distance from the lens to the point where the light rays cross. Does this agree with your earlier measurement of the focal length?

Replace the convex lens with the concave lens. What happens to the light rays?

Larger and Smaller

Placed near an object, a convex lens acts as a magnifying glass. The amount by which it makes things seem bigger depends on the curvature of its sides.

A convex lens will also focus, or bring to a point, the light rays from an object that is far away. The distance from the lens to the point of focus is called the focal length. An object will only be magnified by a convex lens if it lies within the focal length. Exactly the same is true of a concave mirror. Held at a distance from the eye that is greater than the focal length, a convex lens will show distant objects upside down and reduced in size.

A concave lens works in a similar way to a convex mirror. It spreads light rays apart rather than bringing them together, and it makes objects at any distance seem smaller than normal.

CHAPTER 5

Looking into Eyes

Everyone is born with two very important lenses—the lenses of our eyes. Light enters the eye through a small round opening called the pupil. This is the black dot in the middle of your eye. Surrounding the pupil is a circle of muscle known as the iris. Colored chemicals in the iris give it various shades of brown, blue, or green. By altering the size of the pupil, the muscles of the iris control the amount of light that passes into the eyeball.

Just behind the pupil is the

lens. It is flexible like rubber, convex in shape, and small—about the size of your little fingernail. Light, falling on the lens, is focused to form an image on a sort of screen at the back of the eye called the retina. As you move your eyes from distant to near objects, your lenses are pulled from a thin shape to a fatter one by muscles that are attached to them. In this way, whatever you look at can be brought into focus, even though the distance from the lens to the retina stays the same.

The parts of the eye work ▶
together to focus on objects
both nearby and far away.

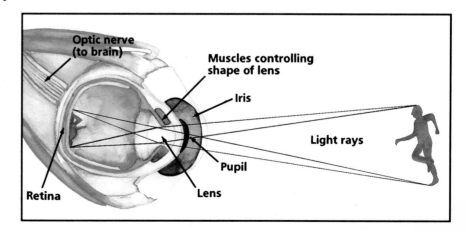

Optic nerve
(to brain)

Muscles controlling
shape of lens

Iris

Light rays

Retina

Pupil

Lens

Eye See!

You Will Need:

- **A mirror**
- **A flashlight**

What to Do:
Partly darken the room, wait about a minute, and look into the mirror. Notice the size of your pupils. Shine the flashlight into one eye. What happens to the pupil of this eye? Notice the movement of the muscles in the iris around the pupil. Turn off the flashlight. How long does it take for your pupil to return to its original size?

Close one eye and hold this page in front of your other eye. Slowly bring the page closer and closer until you can only just see the words clearly. Hold the book in this position for a few seconds, then quickly look up at a distant object. What do you notice? Does the distant object seem clear right away? If not, how long does it take to come into focus? Try to explain the results in terms of what is happening inside your eye. How do you think this affects the ability of your eye to form clear images?

Caution: Eyes are easily damaged. Never press hard on them or stare into bright lights. Never stare at the sun. Looking at the sun through a magnifying glass, binoculars, or telescope can cause permanent blindness within a few seconds.

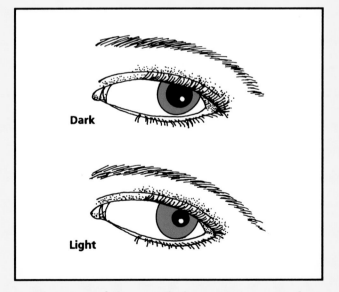

▲ *The size of the pupil changes to control the amount of light entering the eyeball.*

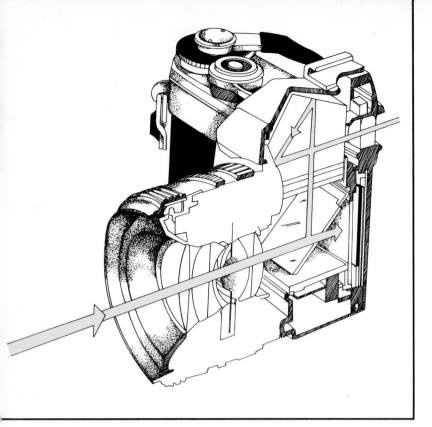

▲ *This cutaway view shows that a camera works in much the same way as a human eye.*

Cameras and Eyes

A camera works almost exactly like a human eye. It, too, uses a convex lens to focus images onto a light-sensitive surface (photographic film). And, just as the eye has a pupil, so the camera has an opening called an aperture that can be widened or narrowed to regulate the amount of light that passes through.

A Model Eye

You Will Need:

- A lamp
- A cardboard box, such as a shoe box
- Black paint and brush
- A sheet of greaseproof paper or other translucent paper
- Sticky tape
- Scissors
- A straight pin

What to Do:

Paint the inside of the box completely black. Cut a square opening on one side and cover this with a piece of greaseproof paper held in place by sticky tape. In the middle of the opposite side, make a tiny hole with a pin. Darken the room except for a single bright lamp. Point the pinhole at the lamp and look at the back of the greaseproof paper. What do you see? Which way up is the image?

The device you have made is known as a pinhole camera. But you can also think of it as being a simple model of an eye. The pinhole serves as both a lens and a pupil. It forms a sharp image because it only lets in light traveling in a single direction from any point on the object.

▲ *The colors of the rainbow.*

Upside-Down World

Incredible though it seems, the images that form on our retinas are upside down. We actually see everything the wrong way up! Fortunately, though, early in life, our brains learn to turn all the images right-side up again to match what we touch and feel. Newborn babies may see everything upside down, but we do not know this for sure. Experiments have also been carried out on people wearing special glasses that turn the images of things upside down. After a

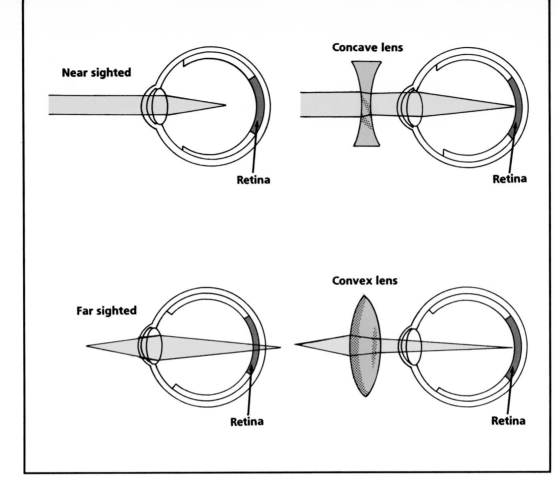

Near sighted

Concave lens

Retina

Retina

Far sighted

Convex lens

Retina

Retina

▲ *These diagrams show how glasses change the direction of light before it enters the eyes of a nearsighted or a farsighted person.*

while, the brains of these people learned to cancel out the effects of the glasses so that the world seemed normal again. But when they took the glasses off, everything looked upside down until their brains once more adjusted!

Help for Eyes

Many people's eyes do not work perfectly. One of the most common problems is when the lens of the eye cannot focus objects clearly on the retina. If the lens is a bit too convex, or highly curved, then it will form images of distant objects that fall in front of the retina. People with this condition are said to be nearsighted because they can see objects clearly only when they are near. The problem is easily solved, however, by wearing glasses with concave lenses. These bend the paths of incoming rays outward slightly to cancel out the overbending of light by the eye lenses. Their exact shape is prescribed by an eye specialist, or optician, after testing the patient's vision.

Another common eye disorder is farsightedness. This occurs when a person can see faraway things clearly but not objects nearby. The solution then is to wear glasses with convex lenses.

Believe It or Not!

IT'S SOMEONE IN THE NEXT TOWN WHO SAYS THE LIGHT IS TOO BRIGHT!

HUMAN EYES ARE SO SENSITIVE THAT, UNDER IDEAL CONDITIONS, WE COULD SEE THE LIGHT FROM A SINGLE CANDLE 16 MILES AWAY.

CHAPTER 6

Over the Rainbow

Our world is filled with color—the green of lush grass, the gray of a heavy mist, the brilliant golds and oranges of sunset. But what is color? How does red light, for instance, differ from violet light?

You can think of light as being a kind of wave, similar to waves in the sea. The distance between one wave crest and the next is known as the wavelength. Different colors of light have different wavelengths. The wavelength of red light is just under one five-thousandth of an inch, while that of violet light is just over one ten-thousandth of an inch. All the other colors fall somewhere in between these two extremes.

These hot-air balloons show different colors of the spectrum of light. ▶

Splitting Sunlight

You Will Need:

- **A large sheet of heavy cardboard**
- **A bowl of water**
- **A flat mirror**
- **A sheet of white cardboard**

What to Do:

Cut a narrow slit in the sheet of heavy cardboard and place it in front of a window on a sunny day. The sun must be shining directly onto the window and you must make sure that light can only get in through the slit. Put the bowl of water on a table behind the cardboard. Hold the mirror at an angle against one side and the sheet of white cardboard above the bowl. Arrange the mirror and cardboard so that a sunbeam falls onto the cardboard. What do you see?

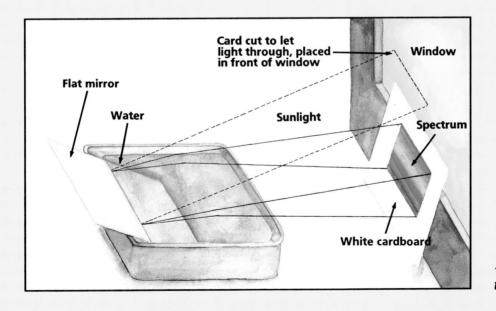

Card cut to let light through, placed in front of window

Window

Flat mirror

Water

Sunlight

Spectrum

White cardboard

◀ *This diagram shows the full spectrum of colors.*

The Spectrum of Colors

Sunlight, or the light from an electric light bulb, seems colorless. We call it "white light." But, in fact, it contains the full range, or spectrum, of colors from red, through orange, yellow, green, blue, and indigo, to violet. When these colors pass from air into water or glass, they are slowed down and refracted by different amounts. Red light is bent the least, violet light the most.

Normally, when white light passes back into air, all its colors are bent back by the same amount so that they join together to make white again. However, if the rays are reflected while still inside the water or glass, they leave by different paths from those by which they entered. In this case, the colors are separated and can be seen as a spectrum from red to violet.

The easiest way to produce a spectrum is with a block of glass called a prism. This has three flat faces running in one direc-

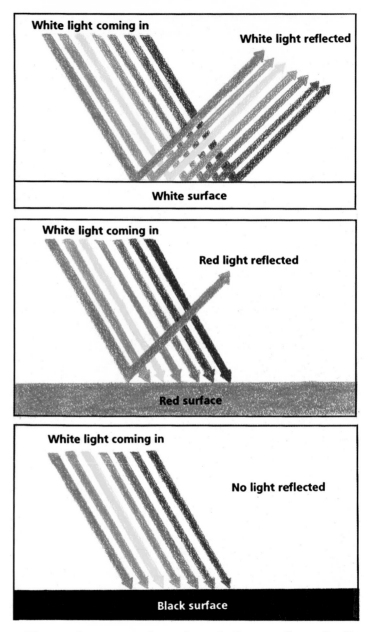

▲ *These drawings show how light is reflected off of a white surface* (top), *a red surface* (middle), *and a black surface* (bottom).

▲ *A rainbow is caused by reflections and refractions of sunlight inside raindrops.*

tion and triangular-shaped ends. However, if conditions are right, white light can also be split apart by other arrangements of glass and by water. A rainbow, for example, is caused by reflections and refractions of sunlight inside raindrops.

What Makes Color?

The colors reflected by an object are those which give it its color. Something that appears white reflects all colors of light. An object that looks red reflects only red light and absorbs all the other colors. Some-

Color Combinations

You Will Need:

- **Three flashlights**
- **Red, green, and blue pieces of cellophane**
- **Three rubber bands**
- **A sheet of white cardboard**

What to Do:

In a well-lit room, hold a piece of red cellophane in front of your eyes. What do you see? What is the normal color of the objects that seem brightest when viewed through the cellophane? What is the normal color of the things that seem darkest?

Make the room as dark as possible and turn on a flashlight. Fix a blue piece of cellophane to the end of the flashlight with a rubber band and again look through the red cellophane. What happens? Look through a piece of blue cellophane, then green. Try different combinations of cellophane in front of your eyes and around the flashlight. Make notes of your findings and try to explain them.

Fasten a piece of red cellophane in front of one flashlight, a blue piece in front of another, and a green piece in front of a third. Darken the room and shine the flashlights onto the cardboard so that their beams overlap. Try the flashlights in pairs and then all three together. What do you notice about the areas where the beams overlap?

Taking It Further:

Repeat the last part of the experiment involving the three flashlights. But this time place your finger in various positions in the beams from the flashlights just before they strike the screen. Look at the different shadows of your finger that are cast. What colors are they? How do you explain what you see?

Note: This experiment will work even better if you use three slide projectors in place of the flashlights, and colored slides instead of cellophane.

thing that appears black absorbs every color and reflects none.

A filter is a material, such as colored cellophane or glass, that only lets light of a particular color pass through. This means that a red object would appear bright when seen through a red filter, but an object of another color would seem dark.

Three of the colors–red, green, and blue–are called primary, because they can be combined in different ways to give every other color. A combination of two primary colors gives a secondary color. Green and red give yellow, green and blue give cyan (a light blue), and blue and red give magenta (light purple).

Tiny Dot Pictures

Look through a magnifying glass at one of the color photos in this book. You will see that the picture is made up from a pattern of tiny dots. Each dot is one of the secondary colors–yellow, cyan, and magenta–or black.

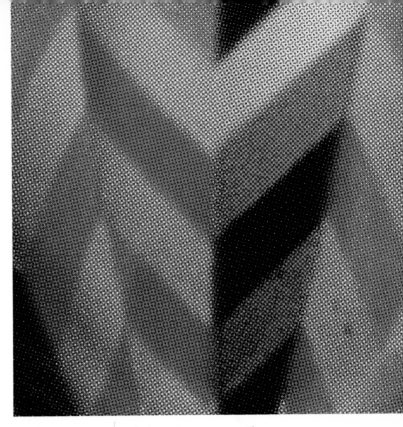

▲ *This photograph has been greatly enlarged so that the tiny dots it is made of are visible.*

Also look through a magnifying glass at the image on a color television screen. Again, the picture is composed of a pattern of tiny dots (or oblongs). Each of the dots is one of the primary colors—red, green, or blue. By rapidly changing the brightness of the dots, any colored moving sequence can be reproduced on the screen.

Eye Sensitivity and Color

You Will Need:

- **A flashlight**
- **Pieces of cellophane of a variety of colors including red, blue, green, yellow, and clear**
- **A rubber band**
- **A book with large print**
- **Several volunteers**

What to Do:

Are human eyes equally sensitive to all colors of light? For example, can we see as much by red light as we can by blue light of the same brightness?

Fix the clear piece of cellophane to the flashlight with the rubber band. Set up the flashlight so that it shines onto an opened page of the book, a fixed distance away. Call in your first subject and ask him or her to stand behind a line marked on the floor on the opposite side of the room. The subject should wait about a minute so that his or her eyes become adjusted to the light level of the room. Then ask the subject to begin slowly moving toward the book until he or she can just read words. Measure the distance between the book and the subject at this point.

Replace the clear cellophane with a colored piece. Ask the subject to return to the starting point, turn to a fresh page, and again allow a minute to pass. Continue the experiment as before. Repeat it using all of the other colored filters. Record your measurements for each filter. Repeat the entire experiment with several other subjects. From your results what do you conclude about the sensitivity of the human eye to different colors?

Taking It Further:

Like all the experiments in this book, this one can be developed further in many ways. For example, you could rearrange it to test how quickly people's eyes recover when exposed to light of different colors. You could do this by shining light of various colors into a subject's eye for a fixed length of time. Then measure how long it is, in each case, before the person can read a book placed some distance away.

Other questions you might investigate: Does eye sensitivity vary with age? Does a person's reaction time depend on the brightness or color of the surrounding light?*

* For more on this, see "Experiment in Depth," pages 54-55, section 5.

Lasers

Special lighting effects play a big part in many of today's live rock concerts. The most spectacular of these effects use laser beams.

A laser is a device that produces a special kind of light. Most ordinary light is a mixture of many colors. But laser light contains just a single wavelength. In ordinary light the waves are out of step with one another and traveling in different directions. But in laser light the waves are all exactly in step and moving along a single, narrow beam.

Laser light is used, among other things, in very high quality printers (laser printers), optical fiber telephone links, and precision cutting and drilling equipment. Lasers have also found their way into hospitals. They make it possible for surgeons to carry out operations using a needle-thin beam of light instead of a knife. Heat from the laser beam seals off any small cut blood vessels quickly. That reduces the amount of blood lost and allows the operation to be completed in less time.

CD Players

Compact disk (CD) players use light in the form of a tiny laser beam to scan the mirrorlike surface of a compact disk. To make a compact disk, the sounds from a studio microphone are first changed into numbers. These numbers are then represented on the surface of a compact disk by a series of tiny pits and blanks. In the player, the CD spins around over a laser beam. When the beam hits a blank or flat part of the disk, it is reflected onto a device called a photocell, which then gives out a small electrical current. But when the beam strikes a pit on the disk, it is scattered and no light reaches the photocell. The resulting electrical signals are amplified, or strengthened, and then used to produce

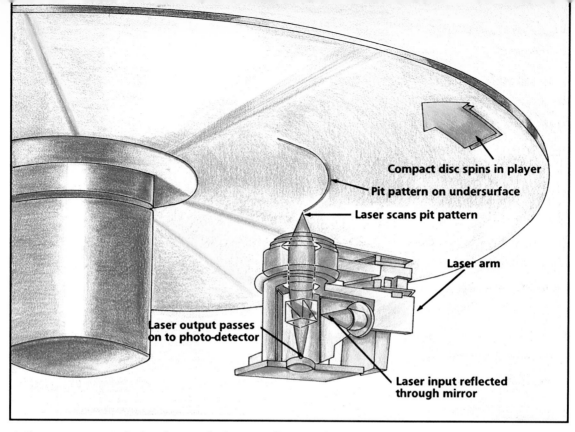

Compact disc spins in player

Pit pattern on undersurface

Laser scans pit pattern

Laser arm

Laser output passes on to photo-detector

Laser input reflected through mirror

▲ *In a compact disk player, light is reflected from the flat part of a disk through a photo-detector.*

sounds from the loudspeakers. Since nothing, except for a beam of light, makes contact with the CD it never wears out and the resulting sound is free of crackles.

Beyond Light

Light is a special type of wave called an electromagnetic wave. But the spectrum of light, from red to violet, forms only a tiny part of the complete electromagnetic spectrum. Other electromagnetic waves include radio waves, X rays, ultraviolet rays, and infrared rays. Ultraviolet rays from the sun, for example, cause sunburn on our skin. We feel the sun's infrared rays, on the other hand, as heat.

All of these invisible kinds of electro-magnetic waves are identical to ordinary light, except in their wavelength. They each have their own uses–in science, medi-cine, and everyday life–and each allows us to view the universe in a new and differ-ent way.

◀ *This giant radio telescope in Puerto Rico detects radio waves from far away in space.*

This section looks at some of the experiments described in this book in more detail.

1. Making Shadows, page 10.
The shadows thrown by an ordinary source of light, such as a lamp or candle, are never completely sharp. What is more, the blurring of the shadow becomes greater as the object is moved nearer to the light. Why should this be?

If a light source were just a point, without any size, then it *would* give perfectly sharp-edged shadows. This situation is shown in the first of the two diagrams below. But ordinary light sources are not just points. They have a definite size. As a result, the shadows they produce consist of two regions. The completely dark central part, where no light from anywhere on the source can get past the object, is called the umbra. Around this is a region of partial shade—the penumbra—into which light from some but not all parts of the source manages to fall. The second of the diagrams shows how this happens.

How does the size ▶ of the light source affect the edge of the shadows in this experiment?

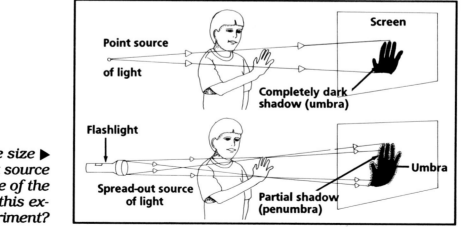

To test these ideas, make a small hole in the middle of a piece of thick cardboard. Then tape the cardboard over your light source so that the hole is exactly over the center of the beam. Observe what effect this has on the shadows that are cast.

2. A Beam Tank, page 18.

It is not easy making beams clearly visible. This is because most of the light is traveling in the direction of the beam and can only be seen by someone looking along that line. The trick is to scatter enough light out of the beam to make it visible from the side without weakening the beam too much. This can be done using very fine particles of matter.

In the "beam tank" described in this chapter, particles of milk, suspended in water, provide the scattering material. An alternative method is to use smoke from a smoldering piece of string or a blown-out candle. But smoke is difficult to work with.

Another problem is to produce rays of light that are bright enough to be seen clearly and that penetrate reasonably far across the tank. It is most important to have an intense source of light such as a slide projector. The positioning of the light source also has an important effect on the quality of the rays in the tank.

Yet another factor is the number, size, and location of the holes in the cardboard that produce the narrow incoming light beams. Finally, it is essential that no stray light enters the observing area as this greatly reduces the visibility of the light beams.

So, there are several aspects to the design and setup of the beam tank that need to be considered carefully. What is the ideal quantity of milk to add to the water? What is the best light source and where should it be placed? What is the most effective pattern and width of holes in the cardboard screen? And so on.

3. Liquid Light, page 23.

The light from the flashlight in this experiment is channeled into the water escaping from the bottom of the bottle. Once inside the stream of water, the light zigzags its way along the flow as it is reflected again and again from the boundary between the water and the air. In this respect, the water acts as an optical fiber. But the fact that you can see the water lit up means that there must be a good deal of light escaping from the sides! Try doing this experiment over a bath or sink in a darkened room so that the water has much farther to fall. What height of water does it take before almost all the light has "leaked" away? You can also try making optical fibers from clear plastic tubing such as that used in aquariums.

4. Reflections in a Spoon, page 25.

The concave side of a spoon will make light rays come together. But it cannot make them all meet exactly at a point. This is because the spoon is curved by different amounts in different places. The center part of the spoon is fairly flat, while parts nearer the edge curve more sharply. Because of this the focal length varies from place to place. By contrast, a specially made concave mirror has a regular curvature all over so that it can focus all incoming light rays to a point.

5. Eye Sensitivity and Color, page 48.

The method described for this experiment is intended only as a guide. A number of improvements could be made. For example, an optician's chart showing letters of different standard sizes would probably work better than a book. Several of these charts (which could be carefully handmade) would be needed, since each subject is to be tested with a number of different colored filters.

Another point to consider is whether

the different filters let through the same amount of light. This could be checked using a light meter.

The experiment would also benefit by some means of making sure that the subject does not lean forward from his or her standing position to see the chart more clearly. An accurate method of measuring the distance from the subject's eyes to the chart is important since the difference in measurements from one filter to the next may not be great.

This is an experiment that could be improved and developed into a lengthy project suitable, say, for a science fair.

aperture—the opening in a camera or eye through which light can enter. Changing the size of the aperture controls the amount of light that can pass through.

compact disk (CD)—a new form of storage for music and other kinds of information. It consists of a metal disk with a mirror-like coating onto which a pattern of tiny pits and blanks is put. This pattern is scanned by a laser inside a CD player.

concave—a concave mirror or lens is one that dips inward from the edge to the center

convex—a convex mirror or lens is one that bulges outward from the edge to the center

density—a measure of how concentrated a piece of matter is. It is equal to the amount of matter, or mass, inside a given volume.

eclipse—the blocking of light from a bright object by something that passes in front of it. Eclipses of the sun are caused by the moon moving between the sun and the earth.

electromagnetic wave—a type of wave that can travel across empty space. Light, radio waves, and X rays are various types of electromagnetic waves, differing only in their wavelength.

energy—a measure of the ability to do work or cause movement

filter—a material that only allows light within a certain range of wavelengths to pass through

focal length—the distance from the center of a mirror or lens to the point at which light rays are brought together (the focus)

image—the appearance of an object formed by a mirror or lens

iris—the colored part of the eye which contains muscles for opening and closing the pupil

laser—a device for producing a very pure, narrow beam of light. Laser light consists of waves of a single wavelength that move exactly in step.

lens—a round, curved piece of transparent material that can be used to focus light or form an image at a particular point

magnify—to increase the apparent size of an object by using one or more curved lenses or mirrors

matter—the stuff of which a thing is made. It may be a solid, liquid, or gas.

opaque—an opaque substance is one that completely stops light from passing through

optical fiber—a specially made strand of glass that allows light to travel through it over long distances

primary color—a color that cannot be made by mixing together other colors of light. There are three primary colors—red, green, and blue.

prism—a solid block of glass, with triangular ends, that can split white light into all the colors of the rainbow

pupil—the tiny opening in the middle of the iris through which light enters the eyeball

reflection—the bouncing back of light from a surface

refraction—the change of direction that a light ray undergoes when it goes from one transparent substance to another

retina—the thin layer at the back of the eye that is sensitive to light

secondary color—a color that can be made by mixing together two of the primary colors of light. There are three secondary colors—yellow, cyan, and magenta.

spectrum—the complete spread of wavelengths of light. It includes all the colors of the rainbow from red to violet.

translucent—a translucent substance is one through which light can pass but which prevents things from being seen clearly

transparent—a transparent substance lets light pass through and objects be seen clearly on the other side

wavelength—the distance from one peak in a series of waves to the next

INDEX

About the Author

Dr. David Darling is the author of many science books for young readers, including the Dillon Press Discovering Our Universe, World of Computers, and Could You Ever? series. Dr. Darling, who holds degrees in physics and astronomy, has also written many articles for *Astronomy* and *Odyssey* magazines. His first science book for adult readers, *Deep Time* (1989), has been described by Arthur C. Clarke as "brilliant." He currently lives with his family in England, where he writes and lectures to students in schools.